D0558681

PRESIDENTIAL

Publications International, Ltd.

CONTENTS

PHILOSOPHIZING 4
ANDREW JOHNSON 12
OXYMORONS 17
RELIGION 22
BARACK OBAMA 28
DEBATABLE ADVICE 33
GREAT ADVICE 36
GOVERNING 41
NATHANIEL HAWTHORNE 51
GOVERNING AMERICA 54
SPECIFICALLY PRESIDENT 60
IN TIMES OF WAR 68
LARGER THAN LIFE 76
FINANCIAL REALTALK 81
SELF EFFACEMENT 89
GEORGE WASHINGTON 98
GETTING OLDER 103
CRINGE HUMOR 107
CLOTHING OPTIONAL 117
ANIMALS 119
INFLATION 126
MIXED BLESSINGS 129
OUCH! 137
ON CLEVELAND POND 148
PARTY TIME 154
HATS OFF 160
LEISURE TIME 164
CHEAP SHOTS 171
CIVILLY DISOBEDIENT 179
FOOD TALK 187

PHILOSOPHIZING

★

No one in the United States is scrutinized so closely as its presidents, whose words — especially after the advent of radio, television, and internet — are often written down for posterity and safekeeping.

Modern politicians are more homogenized in terms of level of education and career (Aaron Sorkin's White House drama The West Wing jokes about its characters almost all having gone to law school), but earlier presidents were farmers and landholders.

All, it turns out, are prone to homilies, "wisdom," and philosophical soundbytes.

"I had heard my father say that he never knew a piece of land run away or break."

— *John Adams*

"Neither a wise man or a brave man lies down on the tracks of history to wait for the train of the future to run over him."

— *Dwight Eisenhower*

"It is infinitely better to have a few good men than many indifferent ones."

— *George Washington*

"It is certainly human to mind your neighbor's business as well as your own. Gossips are only sociologists upon a mean and petty scale."

— *Woodrow Wilson*

"Do not let your bachelor ways crystallize so that you can't soften them when you come to have a wife and a family of your own."

— *Rutherford B. Hayes*

"All my children have spoken for themselves since they first learned to speak, and not always with my advance approval, and I expect that to continue in the future."

— *Gerald Ford*

"I think we consider too much the good luck of the early bird and not enough the bad luck of the early worm."

— *Franklin D. Roosevelt*

"The full ideal is seldom attained."

— *Warren G. Harding*

"If you were on the desert of Sahara, you would feel that you might permit yourself, — well, say, some slight latitude in conduct; but if you saw one of your immediate neighbors coming the other way on a camel, — you would behave yourself until he got out of sight."

— *Woodrow Wilson*

"Better to let him know who's in charge than to let him think he's got the keys to the car."

— *Lyndon B. Johnson*

"A tree is a tree. How many more do you have to look at?"

— *Ronald Reagan*

"Virtue is defined to be mediocrity, of which either extreme is vice."

— *Rutherford B. Hayes*

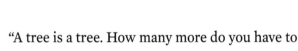

"When one side only of a story is heard and often repeated, the human mind becomes impressed with it insensibly."

— *George Washington*

"Uncompromising thought is the luxury of the closeted recluse."

— *Woodrow Wilson*

"Mr. Hoover, if you see ten troubles coming down the road, you can be sure that nine will run into the ditch before they reach you and you have to battle with only one of them."

— *Calvin Coolidge*

"A pen is certainly an excellent instrument to fix a man's attention and to inflame his ambition."

— *John Adams*

"Truth will do well enough if left to shift for herself. She seldom has received much aid from the power of great men to whom she is rarely known & seldom welcome."

— *Thomas Jefferson*

"Labor disgraces no man; unfortunately you occasionally find men disgrace labor."

— *Ulysses S. Grant*

"The motor car reflects our standard of living and gauges the speed of our present-day life. It long ago ran down Simple Living, and never halted to inquire about the prostrate figure which fell as its victim."

— *Warren G. Harding*

"It is characteristic of the unlearned that they are forever proposing something which is old, and because it has recently come to their own attention, supposing it to be new."

— *Calvin Coolidge*

"Plans are worthless, but planning is everything."

— *Dwight Eisenhower*

ANDREW JOHNSON

Maybe Drunk, Definitely from Tennessee

Abraham Lincoln left enormous (size 13!) shoes to fill, and Andrew Johnson lacked his predecessor's incredible mettle.

Despite his legacy as the tough, stalwart military governor of his home state of Tennessee, Johnson infamously relied on booze to steel himself for the beginning of his term as vice president.

Let's take a deeper look at Johnson's career and reputation leading up to his drunken Senate introduction and troubled presidency.

Andrew Johnson took office after the assassination of Abraham Lincoln, and while he was a disaster as president, he and Lincoln had a political relationship involving mutual trust and reliance. Lincoln supported and advised Johnson, then Tennessee's military governor but previously both a congressman and a senator, as he beat back rebel insurrection and held his state's government together with scant and hard-won shoestrings. Some in Johnson's state even accused him of being Lincoln's puppet:

> "The movement set on foot by the convention and Governor Johnson does not, as seems to be assumed by you, emanate from the National Executive."
>
> — *Abraham Lincoln*

Johnson was a moneyed landowner and slaveowner when Lincoln appointed him military governor. He swore loyalty to the Union and put his money where his mouth was, literally, when the Confederacy took his land and slaves. Though he held views we now find repugnant — he opposed rights for liberated African-Americans and struggled with public, very racist beliefs — those views had evolved quickly and were often set aside in Johnson's service for his nation.

His friends offered to escort him to the statehouse, after postings of a placard saying he should be "shot on sight":

"No, gentlemen, if I am to be shot at, I want no man to be in the way of the bullet."

— *Andrew Johnson, as military governor of Tennessee, asserting that he would walk alone.*

The morning he took the oath as vice president, he drank whiskey and gave an anti-Southern rant. Johnson was too intoxicated to swear in the new senators; a Senate clerk had to handle it.

"The inauguration went off very well except that the Vice President Elect was too drunk to perform his duties and disgraced himself and the Senate by making a drunken foolish speech. I was never so mortified in my life, had I been able to find a hole I would have dropped through it out of sight."

— *Senator Zachariah T. Chandler*

Lincoln defended Johnson, who was not only a tried-and-tested friend to Lincoln and the Union but also an ideal complement for the Republican ticket: Johnson was a pro-Union Democrat.

> "I have known Andy for many years . . . he made a bad slip the other day, but you need not be scared. Andy ain't a drunkard."
>
> — *Abraham Lincoln*

Johnson became more of an . . . *introvert* after his very public run-in with Liquid Courage.

OXYMORONS

★

Our most famous foot-in-mouth president is George W. Bush, but his low-hanging fruit of malapropisms and unintended misstatements only stands out because of frequency.

Other presidents made similar self-contradictory statements in the spirit of famous baseball player and manager Yogi Berra, or they simply stated the obvious as though it were stone-tablet truth.

But sometimes, as Ronald Reagan accidentally pointed out, "Facts are stupid things."

"When more and more people are thrown out of work, unemployment results."

— *Calvin Coolidge*

"I have opinions of my own — strong opinions — but I don't always agree with them."

— *George W. Bush*

"I have had many troubles, but the worst of them never came."

— *James Garfield*

"Things are more like they are now than they ever were before."

— *Dwight Eisenhower*

"There is nothing wrong with America that cannot be cured by what is right with America."

— *Bill Clinton*

"Solutions are not the answer."

— *Richard Nixon*

As president, Ronald Reagan sometimes veered from his written remarks. In 1988, when trying to quote John Adams ("Facts are stubborn things"), Reagan slipped and said, "Facts are stupid things."

★

"When a man is asked to make a speech, the first thing he has to decide is what to say."

— *Gerald Ford*

★

"I have no trouble with my enemies. I can take care of my enemies all right. But my damn friends, my god-damned friends, White, they're the ones who keep me walking the floor nights!"

— *Warren G. Harding, to editor friend William Alan White*

"I rise only to say that I do not intend to say anything."

— *Ulysses S. Grant*

RELIGION

★

Each U.S. president to date is a professed believer in God. Some founding fathers famously were deists, but even these were still versed in the Bible and rejected organized religion or certain specific beliefs.

Almost all presidential speeches conclude with a spin on "God bless America," and presidents have always evoked God and religious belief in both sincerity and gentle jest.

"An atheist is a man who watches a Notre Dame–Southern Methodist University game and doesn't care who wins."

— *Dwight Eisenhower*

"The presidency has a funny way of making a person feel the need to pray."

— *Barack Obama*

"It is not manly to lie even about Satan."

— *James Garfield*

"Business underlies everything in our national life, including our spiritual life. Witness the fact that in the Lord's Prayer, the first petition is for daily bread. No one can worship God or love his neighbor on an empty stomach."

— *Woodrow Wilson*

"I deem the present occasion sufficiently important and solemn to justify me in expressing to my fellow-citizens a profound reverence for the Christian religion and a thorough conviction that sound morals, religious liberty, and a just sense of religious responsibility are essentially connected with all true and lasting happiness; and to that good Being who has blessed us by the gifts of civil and religious freedom, who watched over and prospered the labors of our fathers and has hitherto preserved to us institutions far exceeding in excellence those of any other people, let us unite in fervently commending every interest of our beloved country in all future time."

— a representative sentence (yes, one sentence!) from William Henry Harrison's inaugural speech, during which he is believed to have caught the pneumonia that killed him a month later. He spoke for two hours total and did not wear a coat in the rain. You might think the last president to be born a British subject would have a tougher constitution against the damp.

"He who made us would have been a pitiful bungler, if he had made the rules of our moral conduct a matter of science. For one man of science, there are thousands who are not. What would have become of them?"

— *Thomas Jefferson*

"Which passages of Scripture should guide our public policy? Should we go with Leviticus, which suggests slavery is okay and that eating shellfish is abomination? How about Deuteronomy, which suggests stoning your child if he strays from the faith? Or should we just stick to the Sermon on the Mount — a passage that is so radical that it's doubtful that our own Defense Department would survive its application? So

before we get carried away, let's read our Bibles. Folks haven't been reading their Bibles."

— Barack Obama

"I hope you will be benefitted by your churchgoing. Where the habit does not Christianize, it generally civilizes."

— Rutherford B. Hayes

"Oh, goddammit, we forgot the silent prayer."

— Dwight Eisenhower, leading a cabinet meeting

BARACK OBAMA

Never Metaphor He Didn't Like

President Barack Obama strives to be a populist but his efforts can seem a little strained. His relentless use of metaphors, similes, and analogies isn't usually funny in itself (except maybe "that's a socialist mop") but he uses so many that we could fill a book unto itself.

Fortunately for the writing instructors of the world, he rarely — if ever — mixes his metaphors.

"We don't mind cleaning up the mess that was left for us. We're busy, we got our mops, we're, you know, mopping the floor here. But I don't want the folks who made the mess to just sit there and say, you're not mopping fast enough. I don't want them saying, you're not holding the mop the right way, or, that's a socialist mop. I want them to grab a mop. Grab a mop. Grab a mop — or a broom or something. Make yourself useful."

*— Barack Obama on
the economic recovery*

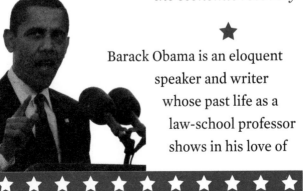

★

Barack Obama is an eloquent
speaker and writer
whose past life as a
law-school professor
shows in his love of

★ ★ ★ ★ ★ ★ ★ ★ ★ ★ ★ ★

analogies and other figurative language. Some are funny on purpose but others are probably attempts to be "relatable" for a chief executive accused of being a socialist mop . . . So to speak.

"A good compromise, a good piece of legislation, is like a good sentence; or a good piece of music. Everybody can recognize it. They say, 'Huh. It works. It makes sense.'"

> — *Barack Obama*

"Contrary to the rumors you have heard, I was not born in a manger. I was actually born on Krypton and sent here by my father Jor-El to save the Planet Earth."

> — *Barack Obama, conjuring Superman lore in response to "birthers"*

"So let's be honest. I need a dance partner here —
and the floor is empty."

— *Barack Obama,*
hesitating on immigration reform

"Michelle will tell you that when we get together
for Christmas or Thanksgiving, it's like a little
mini-United Nations... I've got relatives who look
like Bernie Mac, and I've got relatives who look
like Margaret Thatcher... We've got it all."

— *Barack Obama*

"I've been left at the altar now a couple of times."

— *Barack Obama in debt ceiling negotiations*

"So we might as well do it now — pull off the Band-Aid, eat our peas."

— *Barack Obama in debt ceiling negotiations*

"They call it Armageddon, the end of freedom as we know it. After I signed the bill, I looked around to see if there were any asteroids falling, some cracks opening up in the earth. Turned out it was a nice day."

— *Barack Obama,*
after signing the Affordable Care Act

DEBATABLE
Advice

★

The demographics of U.S. presidents cover a few of our country's most valued humor topics: lawyers, politicians, and dads.

There's also irony in Thomas Jefferson commanding never to bring a book, or Richard Nixon encouraging good, well practiced lying.

Serve this advice chilled and with a grain of salt.

"As to the species of exercise, I advise the gun. While this gives a moderate exercise to the body, it gives boldness, enterprise, and independence to the mind. Games played with the ball, and others of that nature, are too violent for the body, and stamp no character on the mind. Let your gun therefore be the constant companion of your walks. Never think of taking a book with you."

— *Thomas Jefferson*

"If you are resolutely determined to make a lawyer of yourself, the thing is more than half done already."

— *Abraham Lincoln*

"I have found the best way to give advice to your children is to find out what they want and then advise them to do it."

— *Harry S. Truman*

"You'd be surprised how much being a good actor pays off."

— *Ronald Reagan, famous actor*

"You don't know how to lie. If you can't lie, you'll never go anywhere."

— *Richard Nixon, famous liar*

GREAT
Advice

★

Presidency is the pinnacle of U.S. political life and the professed dream career of many children. The men who've occupied the office have had a lot to say about how to live a good, thoughtful life — often with a measured amount of sass.

Whether on education, careers, or etiquette, these chestnuts are entertaining but no less valid for it.

"Be sincere, be brief, be seated."

— Franklin D. Roosevelt

"No man is genuine who is forever trying to pattern his life after the lives of other people, — unless indeed he be a genuine dolt."

— Woodrow Wilson

"Things may come to those who wait, but only the things left by those who hustle."

— Abraham Lincoln

"Do not conceive that fine Clothes make fine Men, any more than fine feathers make fine Birds."

— George Washington

"I will not vote against the truths of the multiplication table."

— James Garfield

"Popularity, I have always thought, may aptly be compared to a coquette—the more you woo her, the more apt is she to elude your embrace."

— John Tyler

"It is better to offer no excuse than a bad one."

— George Washington

"I am rather inclined to silence, and whether that be wise or not, it is at least more unusual nowadays to find a man who can hold his tongue than to find one who cannot."

— *Abraham Lincoln*

"It is possible to tell things by a handshake. I like the 'looking in the eye' syndrome. It conveys interest. I like the firm, though not bone crushing shake. The bone crusher is trying too hard to 'macho it.' The clammy or diffident handshake — fairly or unfairly — get me off to a bad start with a person."

— *George H.W. Bush*

"The purpose of a university should be to make a son as unlike his father as possible. By the time a man has grown old enough to have a son in college he has specialized."

— *Woodrow Wilson*

"While there is nothing in this letter which I shall dread to see in history, it is, perhaps, better for the present that its existence should not become public. I therefore have to request that you will regard it as confidential."

— *Abraham Lincoln*

GOVERNING

★

Presidents have poked fun at themselves and their esteemed office throughout the ages. But they also have spoken extensively on government itself as an idea and an area of potential abuse.

The founding fathers shine in this section — they were the venture capitalists of the startup company of the United States of America. They were making up the great democratic experiment as they went and persuading one another of government's role in American life.

"While all other Sciences have advanced, that of Government is at a stand; little better understood; little better practiced now than three or four thousand years ago."

— *John Adams*

"The other day, someone told me the difference between a democracy and a people's democracy. It's the same difference between a jacket and a straitjacket."

 — *Ronald Reagan*

"I agree with you, Mr. Chairman, that the working men are the basis of all governments, for the plain reason that they are the most numerous."

— *Abraham Lincoln*

"Enlightened statesmen will not always be at the helm."

— *James Madison*

"My brother Bob doesn't want to be in government — he promised Dad he'd go straight."

— *John F. Kennedy*

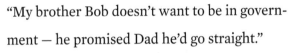

"The thing I enjoyed most were visits from children. They did not want public office."

— *Herbert Hoover*

"If a politician doesn't wanna get beat up, he shouldn't run for office. If a football player doesn't want to get tackled or want the risk of an a occasional clip he shouldn't put the pads on."

— *Bill Clinton*

"A government big enough to give you everything you want is a government big enough to take from you everything you have."

— *Gerald Ford*

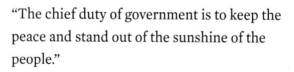

"The chief duty of government is to keep the peace and stand out of the sunshine of the people."

— *James Garfield*

"There are no good laws but such as repeal other laws."

— Andrew Johnson,
unsurprisingly nicknamed "Sir Veto"

"The spirit of resistance to government is so valuable on certain occasions, that I wish it to be always kept alive. It will often be exercised when wrong, but better so than not to be exercised at all. I like a little rebellion now and then. It is like a storm in the atmosphere."

— Thomas Jefferson

"When we are sick, we want an uncommon doctor; when we have a construction job to do, we want an uncommon engineer, and when we are at war, we want an uncommon general. It is only when we get into politics that we are satisfied with the common man."

— *Herbert Hoover*

"Patriotism means to stand by the country.

It does not mean to stand by the president."

— *Theodore Roosevelt*

"A popular Government without popular information, or the means of acquiring it, is but a Prologue to a Farce or a Tragedy, or perhaps both."

— *James Madison*

"I have always said that my whole public life was an experiment to determine whether an intelligent people would sustain a man in acting sensibly on each proposition that arose, and in doing nothing for mere show or demagogical effect."

— James Garfield. President Garfield was only nominated by the Republican Party after thirty-five failed rounds of ballots at the 1880 convention. No one will ever know how many of those rounds were for mere show.

"If you think too much about being re-elected, it is very difficult to be worth re-electing."

— Woodrow Wilson

"It is senseless to boast of our liberty when we find that to so shocking an extent it is merely the liberty to go ill-governed."

— *Calvin Coolidge*

"I know no method to secure the repeal of bad or obnoxious laws so effective as their stringent execution."

— *Ulysses S. Grant*

"Voting's the best revenge."

— *Barack Obama*

"I have a different vision of leadership. A leadership is someone who brings people together."

— *George W. Bush*

"I met a very engaging young fellow who introduced himself to me as the mayor of the town, and added that he was a Socialist. I said, 'What does that mean? Does that mean that this town is socialistic?' 'No, sir,' he said; 'I have not deceived myself; the vote by which I was elected was about 20 per cent. socialistic and 80 per cent. protest.'"

— *Woodrow Wilson*

"There are some who lack confidence in the integrity and capacity of the people to govern themselves. To all who entertain such fears I will most respectfully say that I entertain none... If a man is not capable, and is not to be trusted with the government of himself, is he to be trusted with the government of others... Who, then, will govern? The answer must be, Man — for we have no angels in the shape of men, as yet, who are willing to take charge of our political affairs."

— Andrew Johnson

"It is much more important to kill bad bills than to pass good ones."

— Calvin Coolidge

NATHANIEL
Hawthorne

★

The dark Romantic writer most famous for his novel The Scarlet Letter *wrote an 1852 biography of Franklin Pierce that didn't exactly tell the whole truth and nothing but the truth.*

Pierce was an otherwise un-noteworthy president whose friend Hawthorne noted in the book:

> *"The author of this memoir—being so little of a politician that he scarcely feels entitled to call himself a member of any party—would not voluntarily have undertaken the work here offered to the public."*

Any student in the United States who was ever made to read Nathaniel Hawthorne's *The Scarlet Letter* — or who watched a movie version instead — knows the writer to be a purveyor of dark moral warnings. But Hawthorne did a nigh unrecognizable about-face when he wrote a loving, maybe even fawning, biography of his friend Franklin Pierce.

The two men were born the same year and met as teens, and the lifelong friendship between them was real. Less real was the version of Pierce presented in Hawthorne's biography, which was timed to coincide with the 1852 presidential election.

"This frankness, this democracy of good feeling, has not been chilled by the society of politicians," Hawthorne wrote, in one of many rosy depictions of Pierce's general lack of having distinguished himself in almost any way — besides being anti-abolition.

Hawthorne himself admits he's out of his comfort zone writing nonfiction (*ahem*) about an old friend. Of course, money talks, and Hawthorne was richly rewarded with a lucrative foreign position in the Pierce administration.

GOVERNING
America

★

One requirement of the presidency is constant thoughtful praise of the United States. More than that, presidents evoke the spirit of America when they make sweeping, aspirational speeches.

Often these speeches create a straw man who criticizes America and the president rebukes him. But the founding fathers used their funny or witty comments to move one another to write policy.

Still others are cutting criticisms of politics and American government.

"But America is a great, unwieldy Body. Its Progress must be slow. It is like a large Fleet sailing under Convoy. The fleetest Sailors must wait for the dullest and slowest. Like a Coach and six — the swiftest Horses must be slackened and the slowest quickened, that all may keep an even Pace."

— John Adams

"If anyone tells you America's best days are behind her, they're looking the wrong way."

— George H.W. Bush

"Whenever you hear a man prating about the Constitution, spot him as a traitor."

— Andrew Johnson

"What did you expect? I don't know why we're so surprised. When you put your foot on a man's neck and hold him down for three hundred years, and then you let him up, what's he going to do? He's going to knock your block off."

— *Lyndon B. Johnson on the struggle for civil rights*

⭐

"As a nation we may take pride in the fact that we are softhearted; but we cannot afford to be soft-headed."

— *Franklin D. Roosevelt*

⭐

"The nine most terrifying words in the English language are: 'I'm from the government and I'm here to help.'"

— *Ronald Reagan*

"Unlike any other nation, here the people rule, and their will is the supreme law. It is sometimes sneeringly said by those who do not like free government, that here we count heads. True, heads are counted, but brains also."

— *William McKinley*

"The passion for office among members of Congress is very great, if not absolutely disreputable, and greatly embarrasses the operations of the government. They create offices by their own votes and then seek to fill them themselves."

— *James K. Polk*

"We don't propose to sit here in our rocking chair with our hands folded and let the Communists set up any government in the Western Hemisphere."

— *Lyndon B. Johnson*

"I knew that my staying up would not change the election result if I were defeated, while if elected I had a hard day ahead of me. So I thought a night's rest was best in any event."

— *Benjamin Harrison, who went to bed early and slept soundly the night after the 1888 presidential election*

"And you know, it's kind of an American tradition to show a certain skepticism toward our democratic institutions. I myself have sometimes thought the aging process could be delayed if it had to make its way through Congress."

— *George H.W. Bush*

"F--- your parliament and your constitution. America is an elephant. Cyprus is a flea. Greece is a flea. If these two fleas continue itching the elephant, they may just get whacked good."

— *Lyndon B. Johnson*

"The Declaration of Independence I always considered as a Theatrical Show. Jefferson ran away with all the stage effect of that; i.e. all the Glory of it."

— *John Adams*

SPECIFICALLY
President

★

Each president's memorial or presidential library should feature its namesake's official remark on what it means to be president.

These comments are as funny as they are truthful. Of course, for our more modern presidents, keep the old adage in mind: Behind every great president is a great . . . speechwriter.

"My movements to the chair of Government will be accompanied by feelings not unlike those of a culprit who is going to the place of his execution: so unwilling am I, in the evening of a life nearly consumed in public cares, to quit a peaceful abode for an Ocean of difficulties."

— *George Washington*

"Any man who wants to be president is either an egomaniac or crazy."

— *Dwight Eisenhower*

"Being president is like running a cemetery: You've got a lot of people under you and nobody's listening."

— *Bill Clinton*

"There are blessed intervals when I forget by one means or another that I am President of the United States."

— *Woodrow Wilson*

"No man who ever held the office of president would congratulate a friend on obtaining it. He will make one man ungrateful, and a hundred men his enemies, for every office he can bestow."

— *John Adams*

"Many years ago, I concluded that a few hair shirts were part of the mental wardrobe of every man. The president differs from other men in that he has a more extensive wardrobe."

— *Herbert Hoover*

"The President is the last person in the world to know what the people really want and think."

— *James Garfield*

"Madam, I may be President of the United States, but my private life is nobody's damn business."

— *Chester A. Arthur, definitely not a psychic*

⭐

"I have come to the conclusion that the major part of the work of a President is to increase the gate receipts of expositions and fairs and bring tourists to town."

— *William Howard Taft*

⭐

"I never wanted to get out of a place as much as I did to get out of the presidency."

— Ulysses S. Grant

"I think the American people want a solemn ass as a President and I think I will go along with them."

— Calvin Coolidge, "Silent Cal," who nonetheless delivered countless sharp one liners

"If one morning I walked on top of the water across the Potomac River, the headline that afternoon would read: 'President Can't Swim.'"

— Lyndon B. Johnson

"I can say that never in the last fifteen years have I had the peace of mind that I have since the election. I have almost a feeling of elation."

> — *Herbert Hoover, on losing the 1932 presidential election*

★

"The people can never understand why the President does not use his powers to make them behave. Well all the president is, is a glorified public relations man who spends his time flattering, kissing, and kicking people to get them to do what they are supposed to do anyway."

> — *Harry S. Truman*

★

"The Presidency, even to the most experienced politicians, is no bed of roses; and General Taylor, like others, found thorns within it."

— Abraham Lincoln, eulogizing
Zachary Taylor in 1850

★

"I don't think any President ever enjoyed himself more than I did. Moreover, I don't think any ex-President ever enjoyed himself more."

— Theodore Roosevelt

★

"There is one thing about being President — nobody can tell you when to sit down."

— Dwight Eisenhower

★

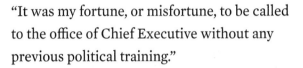

"With me it is emphatically true that the presidency is 'no bed of roses.'"

— *James K. Polk*

"It was my fortune, or misfortune, to be called to the office of Chief Executive without any previous political training."

— *Ulysses S. Grant*

"My country has in its wisdom contrived for me the most insignificant office that ever the invention of man contrived or his imagination conceived."

— *John Adams, when vice president*

IN TIMES
Of War

★

War is not funny. But it was vital to the creation and sustenance of the United States of America.

As a result, dark humor is an integral part of our landscape, and many presidents served in the military conflicts that inspire this dark humor. Their remarks on the topic are often confined to letters and diaries meant for private use or loved ones at home.

All are meant with utmost respect.

"Wars produce many stories of fiction, some of which are told until they are believed to be true."

— *Ulysses S. Grant*

During the Civil War, Lieutenant Colonel Oliver Wendell Holmes once spotted an exceptionally tall civilian standing on the parapet. Holmes yelled, "Get down, you damn fool!" Much to his surprise, the man was Abraham Lincoln, and Lincoln cheerfully complied with the order.

"Fighting battles is like courting girls: those who make the most pretensions and are boldest usually win."

— *Rutherford B. Hayes*

"The men think I am not much afraid of shells but they don't know. I was too scared to run and that is pretty scared."

— *Harry S. Truman, writing home about his command of a battery unit in World War I.*

"I know we are in frequent perils, that we may never return and all that, but the feeling that I am where I ought to be is a full compensation for all that is sinister, leaving me free to enjoy as if on a pleasure tour."

— *Rutherford B. Hayes*

"I have just read your despatch about sore-tongued and fatigued horses. Will you pardon me for asking what the horses of your army have done since the battle of Antietam that fatigues anything?"

— Abraham Lincoln,
to General George McClellan

James Buchanan sent a federal army to assert authority over the unruly Utah territory. The war was immensely unpopular with the American public, who considered the entire expedition unnecessary and expensive. Buchanan was happy to resolve it in 1858. Aside from destroyed property, the Utah War, or "Buchanan's Blunder" as it was called, ended without a single pitched battle.

"There is nothing that will make an Englishman s--- so quick as the sight of General Washington." — the punchline of a story Abraham Lincoln liked to tell about war hero Ethan Allen seeing a portrait of Washington hung in a British outhouse

★

"We have dancing ... from soon after sundown until a few minutes after nine o'clock.... Occasionally the boys who play the female partners in the dances exercise their ingenuity in dressing to look as girlish as possible. In the absence of lady duds they use leaves, and the leaf-clad beauties often look very pretty and always odd enough."

— *Rutherford B. Hayes*

"If you are besieged, how do you despatch me?
Why did you not leave before being besieged?"

— *Abraham Lincoln*

"My only objection to the arrangements there is
the two-in-a-bed system. It is bad.... But let your
words and conduct be perfectly pure — such
as your mother might know without bringing a
blush to your cheek.... If not already mentioned,
do not tell your mother of the doubling in bed."

— *Rutherford B. Hayes*

"Oh, I am heartily tired of hearing about what Lee is going to do. Some of you always seem to think he is suddenly going to turn a double somersault, and land in our rear and on both of our flanks at the same time. Go back to your command, and try to think what we are going to do ourselves, instead of what Lee is going to do."

— *Ulysses S. Grant*

"General Grant is a copious worker and fighter, but a very meager writer or telegrapher. No doubt he changed his purpose in regard to the Ninth Corps for some sufficient reason, but has forgotten to notify us of it." — Abraham Lincoln, who one August 9 wrote to Ulysses S. Grant to ask, "Did you receive a short letter from me dated 13th of July?"

"When the weather is bad as it was yesterday, everybody, almost everybody, feels cross and gloomy. Our thin linen tents — about like a fish seine, the deep mud, the irregular mails, the never to-be-seen paymasters, and "the rest of mankind," are growled about in "old-soldier" style. But a fine day like today has turned out brightens and cheers us all. We people in camp are merely big children, wayward and changeable."

— *Rutherford B. Hayes*

LARGER
Than Life

★

With a schedule stuffed with diverse hobbies and a long, varied political life, Theodore Roosevelt became a cult of personality long before his death and moreso after it.

Roosevelt and his cousin, the more bookish and effete Franklin Delano Roosevelt, formed a yin and yang of American political life — even from opposite parties.

But FDR wasn't short on toughness or leadership, and Teddy wasn't short on brains or foresight. He just happened to be a charismatic adventurer, too.

Theodore Roosevelt had many memorable nicknames. Teddy Roosevelt was known as "The Trustbuster," who broke up giant corporations, and "The Rough Rider," whose wartime heroics in Cuba made him "The Hero of San Juan Hill." Yet Roosevelt was also cruelly dubbed "Old Four Eyes" for his pronounced myopia and "The Meddler" for his intervention in many sectors of society. He continued to work in national politics until his death in 1919.

Many historians agree that the 26th president had more hobbies than any president before or since. "TR" enjoyed the outdoors and relished hunting and exploring. Roosevelt also enjoyed

reading, writing, and ornithology. When he
briefly soured on politics in the 1910s, he
explored the Amazon instead. It's hard to say
which is a more harrowing life path.

Roosevelt was shot as he campaigned for the
presidency in 1912. The bullet hit him in the chest
but not before passing through his glasses case
and the folded speech in his pocket. Roosevelt
received a superficial wound and finished his
speech before going to the hospital for treatment
90 minutes later.

While Calvin Coolidge, Franklin D. Roosevelt,
and Richard Nixon were also rumored to be pro-
astrology, Theodore Roosevelt let it all hang out

when he signed on as a founding member of the American Society for Psychic Research. (The only later president who was so card-carryingly astrological was Ronald Reagan, whose wife Nancy famously made him both a Republican and a believer in psychics. Strange bedfellows.)

You can thank Roosevelt for his help in spreading the myth of the piranha as a relentless, bloodthirsty carnivore. During his trip through Brazil in 1913, Roosevelt witnessed a piranha feeding frenzy that caused him to label the fish "the embodiment of evil ferocity."

But according to historians, Roosevelt was the victim of a setup. A local ichthyologist blocked off a section of river with nets and stocked it with

thousands of pole-caught piranha, which were left unfed for several days.

When Roosevelt and his entourage arrived by boat, they were warned not to stick their hands in the water because of the vicious fish that lived there. Skeptical, Roosevelt and the journalists who were with him demanded proof, so an ailing cow was driven into the water, where it was immediately devoured by the starving piranha.

Roosevelt was awestruck and he went home with a tale of terror that remains popular to this day, inspiring countless movies, documentaries, and campfire tales.

It's definitely a myth. Go ahead, take a swim.

FINANCIAL
Realtalk

★

A surprising amount of American history is filled with strong, constant debate over abstract economics: tariffs, the gold standard, hard money, or something called "specie."

But the broad strokes of remarks on the economy are always the same. To deficit or not to deficit? Will a minimum wage sink the private sector? What's the best way to counter a recession?

Herbert Hoover shines in this section, though that may not be the right word to use.

"I regard the inflation acts as wrong in all ways. Personally I am one of the noble army of debtors, and can stand it if others can. But it is a wretched business."

— Rutherford B. Hayes

"The way to stop financial joy-riding is to arrest the chauffeur, not the automobile."

— Woodrow Wilson

"I am not worried about the deficit. It is big enough to take care of itself."

— Ronald Reagan

Chester A. Arthur thought the White House was out-of-date and gloomy, so he replaced 24 wagonloads of old furniture with new items. Relatedly, he was called "Prince Arthur" due to his weakness for fine clothes and accommodations.

"Do not let any calamity-howling executive with an income of $1,000 a day [...] tell you that a wage of $11.00 a week is going to have a disastrous effect on all American industry."

— Franklin D. Roosevelt, before signing the first federal minimum wage into law. Eleven dollars a week is equivalent to less than $200 today.

"When your economy is kind of ooching along, it's important to let people have more of their own money."

> — *George W. Bush . . . As though any other president could have said "ooching."*

"A boss is a much more formidable master than a king, because a king is an obvious master, whereas the hands of the boss are always where you least expect them to be."

> — *Woodrow Wilson*

"The existence of this motto on the coins was a constant source of jest and ridicule; and this was unavoidable. Everyone must remember the innumerable cartoons and articles based on phrases like 'In God we trust for the other eight cents'; 'In God we trust for the short weight'; 'In god we trust for the thirty-seven cents we do not pay'; and so forth and so forth."

— *Theodore Roosevelt*

"The bank, Mr. Van Buren, is trying to kill me, but I will kill it."

— *Andrew Jackson*

"My wants are many, and, if told,
Would muster many a score;
And were each wish a mint of gold,
I still would want for more."

— *John Quincy "Old Man Eloquent" Adams*

"It's a recession when your neighbor loses his job; it's a depression when you lose yours."

— *Harry S. Truman*

"About the time we can make the ends meet, somebody moves the ends."

— *Herbert Hoover*

"He asked me, smiling, if I thought it too vast and anti-republican a privilege for the ex-presidents to have their letters and newspapers free, considering that this was the only earthly benefit they carried away from their office."

— *political sociologist Harriet Martineau, describing a meeting with elderly James Madison in Retrospect of Western Travel*

"You do not take a man who for years has been hobbled by chains, liberate him, bring him to the starting line of a race, saying, 'you are free to compete with all the others,' and still justly believe you have been completely fair."

— *Lyndon B. Johnson, speaking at Howard University, one of the Historically Black Colleges and Universities*

"Things may be too cheap. [...] I pity the man who wants a coat so cheap that the man or woman who produces the cloth or shapes it into a garment will starve in the process."

— *Benjamin Harrison*

"Blessed are the young for they shall inherit the national debt."

— *Herbert Hoover*

SELF EFFACEMENT

★

Presidents are the best in the land at reminding us how human they really are. Unfortunately, they usually do it through their actions, but sometimes they make fun of themselves on purpose. Only sometimes are they also trying to be funny.

These jokes again fall into broad categories well represented by our presidents to date: uncool dads, young whippersnappers, or . . . being pretty bad presidents. It's amazing how different these remarks sound when delivered to a sympathetic audience at a party's national convention.

"Thanks to God that he gave me stubbornness when I know I am right."

— *John Adams*

"You have to admit that in my sentences I go where no man has gone before. I've coined new words, like 'misunderstanding.'"

— *George W. Bush, mocking his own, um, lexigacy*

"I have not permitted myself, gentlemen, to conclude that I am the best man in the country; but I am reminded in this connection of a story of an old Dutch farmer, who remarked to a companion once that it was not best to swap horses when crossing a stream."

— *Abraham Lincoln*

"I am a Ford, not a Lincoln."

— Gerald Ford

"I am not fit for this office and should never have been here."

— "Wobbly" Warren G. Harding

"Most of all, I want to thank you for all the generous advance coverage you've given me in anticipation of a successful career. When I actually do something, we'll let you know."

— Barack Obama at the 2006 Gridiron Club Dinner (. . . Or the Nobel Peace Prize committee? Zing.)

"If I had another face, do you think I would wear this one?"

— Abraham Lincoln, accused of being "two-faced" by Stephen Douglas

"A lot of presidential memoirs, they say, are dull and self-serving. I hope mine is interesting and self-serving."

— Bill Clinton

"My speaking is irregular. Sometimes quite good, sometimes not, but generally will do... I am too far along in experience and years both for this business. I do not go into [it] with the zest of old times. Races, baseball, and politics are for the youngsters."

— Rutherford B. Hayes

"I am trying to do two things: dare to be a radical and not be a fool, which, if I may judge by the exhibitions around me, is a matter of no small difficulty."

— *James Garfield*

"After I received the news, Malia walked in and said, 'Daddy, you won the Nobel Peace Prize, and it is Bo's birthday!' And then Sasha added, 'Plus, we have a three-day weekend coming up.' So it's good to have kids to keep things in perspective."

— *Barack Obama*

"I have now come to the conclusion never again to think of marrying, and for this reason; I can never be satisfied with anyone who would be blockhead enough to have me."

— *Abraham Lincoln*

"And we believe very strongly on preserving the right to differ in this country, and the right to dissent; and if I have done a good job of anything since I've been president, it's to ensure that there are plenty of dissenters."

— *Lyndon B. Johnson*

"Well, first of all, let me say that I have never used Twitter. I noticed that young people — they're very busy with all these electronics. My thumbs are too clumsy to type in things on the phone."

— *Barack Obama*

"All of you know I'm having to become quite an expert in this business of asking for forgiveness."

— *Bill Clinton*

"I can't deny I'm a better ex-president than I was a president."

— *Jimmy Carter*

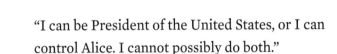

"I can be President of the United States, or I can control Alice. I cannot possibly do both."

— *Theodore Roosevelt, accurately summing his daughter Alice's capacity to make trouble.*

"Do they think that I am such a damned fool as to think myself fit for President of the United States? No, sir; I know what I am fit for. I can command a body of men in a rough way, but I am not fit to be President."

— *Andrew Jackson*

"I long for rural and domestic scenes, for the warbling of Birds and the Prattle of my Children. Don't you think I am somewhat poetical this morning, for one of my Years, and considering the Gravity, and Insipidity of my Employment?"

— *John Adams*

"I am the first to admit that I am no great orator or no person that got where I have gotten by any William Jennings Bryan technique."

— *Gerald Ford, referring to the famously well spoken former candidate*

"I feel as if it were time for me to write to someone who will believe what I write."

— *Grover Cleveland, in an 1892 letter to his brother*

"I only know two tunes. One is Yankee Doodle, and the other one isn't."

— *Ulysses S. Grant*

GEORGE WASHINGTON
Humble spendthrift

★

Our most accomplished military leader and hesitant first president took no wage, but he used his expense account in a thoroughly modern way.

He spent thousands and thousands of dollars on food and alcohol for himself — not his troops or fellow Americans, who were for the most part not wealthy landowners like Washington.

But the gravy train eventually came to a stop.

"As to pay, Sir, I beg leave to assure the Congress that as no pecuniary consideration could have tempted me to accept this arduous employment at the expense of my domestic ease and happiness, I do not wish to make any profit from it."

— *George Washington, big talker*

When Washington took over the Continental Army in 1775, George Washington refused to accept a salary. Perhaps he did so to demonstrate sacrifice and solidarity with the "have-nots," a group that included soldiers under his command. Many  praised Washington without knowing that he had carte blanche to use government funds.

From September 1775 to March 1776, Washington spent more than $6,000 on alcohol alone. And during the harsh Valley Forge winter of 1777–78, while his troops died of hunger and exposure, Washington indulged his appetite. An expense-account entry included "geese, mutton, fowls, turkey, veal, butter, turnips, potatoes, carrots, and cabbage."

> "If there are spots in his character, they are like the spots in the Sun; only discernable by the magnifying powers of a telescope."
>
> — *Francis Hopkinson, a Declaration signer who definitely wasn't a bookkeeper*

By 1783, Washington had spent almost $450,000 on food, saddles, clothing, accommodations, and sundries. In today's dollars, that's $5 million.

When he became president, Washington again offered to waive his salary in favor of an expense account. The offer was politely refused, and he was paid a $25,000 stipend. It seems America could no longer afford the general's brand of sacrifice.

"All see the glare which hovers round the external trappings of elevated office. To me there is nothing in it, beyond the lustre which may be reflected from its connection with a power of promoting human felicity."

— *George Washington in 1790*
. . . having received his new paycheck?

Originally the title of the leader of the United States was supposed to be "His Highness the President of the United States of America and

Protector of the Rights of the Same." Washington, however, disliked the use of "His Highness" and settled upon simply "Mr. President."

(When Vice President John Adams suggested that Washington be referred to as "His Majesty," Adams's foes responded with his own honorific: "His Rotundity.")

Fortunately, Washington's humility about his title suited the end of his king's-ransom expense account. But abuse of public funds for lavish meals and other personal use is still a prominent part of political life in these United States.

GETTING
Older

★

Life expectancy is a hard number to pin down, but U.S. presidents have loved to joke at the expense of their own advancing ages.

Ronald Reagan was the oldest president to serve and his actorly zest for jokes helped him talk about his age without categorizing it as a weakness.

Other presidents, like James Madison, darkly joked about their perceived slide into aged irrelevance.

"A man whose years have but reached the canonical three-score-&-ten (and mine are much beyond the number) should distrust himself, whether distrusted by his friends or not, and should never forget that his arguments, whatever they may be will be answered by allusions to the date of his birth."

— *James Madison*

"I must do something to keep my thoughts fresh and growing. I dread nothing so much as falling into a rut and feeling myself becoming a fossil."

— *James Garfield*

"When I go in for a physical, they no longer ask how old I am. They carbon date me."

— *Ronald Reagan*

"In the last few days of this past monumentous year, our family was blessed once more, celebrating the joy of life when a little boy became our twelfth grandchild. When I held the little guy for the first time, the troubles at home and abroad seemed manageable, and totally in perspective. And now I know, I know you're probably thinking, Well, that's just a grandfather talking."

— *George H.W. Bush*

"I am tired of being under age in politics. I don't want to be associated with anybody except those who are politically over twenty-one."

— *Woodrow Wilson*

"This fellow they've nominated claims he's the new Thomas Jefferson. Well, let me tell you something. I knew Thomas Jefferson. He was a friend of mine. And governor, you're no Thomas Jefferson."

> — *Ronald Reagan, mocking his own "advanced age" in a jab at Democratic presidential nominee Bill Clinton*

"Nor, indeed, with more time, could I have added much to it that would not have been superfluous to you, as well as inconvenient at the octogenary age of which I am reminded whenever I take up my pen on such subjects."

> — *James Madison*

CRINGE HUMOR

★

As with oxymorons, George W. Bush seems like the natural standout for presidential cringe humor.

But he isn't alone, not by a long stretch. Cringeable topics range from very young wives to international ignorance to dubious praise from elsewhere.

Bill Clinton holds the distinction of most cringey personal behaviors in recent memory. Controversial presidents like Warren G. Harding are thankful in absentia that they didn't govern in the internet age.

"No, I didn't read the budget. I hired people to read the budget."

— George W. Bush

"I'm only waiting for my wife to grow up."

— Grover Cleveland, whose future wife, Frances Folsom, was 9 years old at the time. True to his word, he wed Folsom in the Blue Room of the White House on June 2, 1886, an event that turned Folsom into the youngest first lady in our nation's history: Cleveland was 49 years old, Folsom was 21.

"Youth, however, is a defect that she is fast getting away from and may perhaps be entirely rid of before I shall want her."

— Rutherford B. Hayes, about Lucy Webb, nine years his junior, whom he later married.

"For seven and a half years I've worked alongside President Reagan. We've had triumphs. Made some mistakes. We've had some sex...uh... setbacks."

— *George H.W. Bush*

Jimmy Carter told reporters that he once saw what could have been a UFO, before he was governor of Georgia. "It was the darndest thing I've ever seen," he said of the incident. Carter was often referred to as "the UFO president."

"No one wants to get this matter behind us more than I do — except maybe all the rest of the American people."

— *Bill Clinton on the Monica Lewinsky scandal*

Ulysses S. Grant was known as "Unconditional Surrender" for his leadership in the Civil War. But as president he was derided as "Useless" Grant.

"Awesome speech!"

— *George W. Bush, praising Pope Benedict XVI*

Calvin Coolidge enjoyed having his head massaged with Vaseline petroleum jelly while he ate breakfast — presumably because this tidbit would make anyone lose their lunch.

"We in America today are nearer to the final triumph over poverty than ever before in the history of any land."

— *Herbert Hoover, definitely not a psychic, in 1928*

"Free nations are peaceful nations. Free nations don't attack each other. Free nations don't develop weapons of mass destruction."

— *George W. Bush*

"Well, I learned a lot. ... You'd be surprised. They're all individual countries."

— *Ronald Reagan on Latin America*

During a microphone test before a 1984 radio address, Ronald Reagan said, "My fellow Americans, I am pleased to tell you I just signed legislation which outlaws Russia forever. The bombing begins in five minutes." Orson Welles had nothing nice to say about President Reagan but they both belong to the Radio Disaster Hall of Fame.

"Rarely is the question asked, is our children learning?"

— *George W. Bush, whose error made some wonder if he was Left Behind in grammar class.*

"He erred from limitation of grasp and perception, perhaps, or through sore perplexity in trying times, but never weakly or consciously. He was always headstrong and 'sure he was right' even in his errors."

— The New York Times, *in its obituary for President Andrew Johnson*

★

"I am very sure we shall have no conflict of opinion about constitutional duties or authority."

— *Warren G. Harding, definitely not a psychic*

★

"As yesterday's positive report card shows, childrens do learn when standards are high and results are measured."

— *George W. Bush*

While president, Lyndon B. Johnson had his gallbladder and a stone from his ureter removed. During a post-surgery press conference, Johnson lifted his pajama top to show his 12-inch scar.

★

Former actor Ronald Reagan was the only U.S. president ever to wear a Nazi uniform, having done so for a film role. This accident of fate is funny and a little cringeworthy. But Woodrow Wilson's published sympathies for the Ku Klux Klan were prominently quoted in the 1915 revisionist history epic *Birth of a Nation* and he agreed to screen the film at the White House — a totally humorless series of events.

★

"What the country needs is a good big laugh."

— Herbert Hoover

"If some one could get off a good joke every ten days, I think our troubles would be over."

— Herbert Hoover

"His iron will and unflinching spirit did not permit him to falter in attempting to perform what his conscience and his sense of duty impelled him to achieve, though his task be accompanied by disaster to his country, the wreck of his party, and, before the end, the literal shrieks of his fellow-men."

— The Press, *London, on Grover Cleveland*

After abruptly ending a press conference in China, President George W. Bush exited stage right — only to find his escape hampered by a locked door. Despite his tugging at the door and mugging for the cameras, Bush was at a loss until an aide escorted him from the room.

CLOTHING
Optional

John Quincy Adams isn't known for much besides his daily nude swims. In fact, his habit led to a milestone of women's rights, purely by accident.

There are more jokes to be made about how he was given an alligator by a foreign leader or how it's fortunate that Theodore Roosevelt's piranha excursion wasn't in the Potomac River.

But presidents deserve our respect.

John Quincy Adams regularly swam nude in the Potomac River at 5:00 a.m. He took his last swim on his 79th birthday.

In the 1820s, Anne Royall secured the first interview granted to a female reporter by a U.S. president by refusing to give John Quincy Adams his clothes after one of his swims.

Totally unrelatedly, Adams was the first president to be photographed.

ANIMALS

★

The presidential pardon of a Thanksgiving turkey is a well known tradition, and the Obama family's selection of their White House dog, Bo, was a news story for a (cringeworthy?) number of days.

But the White House has always been full of animals ranging from pets to exotic gifts. When you send a herd of elephants, isn't it polite to also send a shelter for them and some handlers?

At least there was only one runaway goat.

Animal species named in honor of Barack Obama include a puffbird, a lichen, an extinct lizard, and a wafer trapdoor spider.

⭐

Upon receiving a raccoon for his Thanksgiving dinner, Calvin Coolidge promptly named her Rebecca. Rebecca had an annoying habit: unscrewing lightbulbs as she wandered through the White House. If only she'd been skilled in the ways of Coolidge's favorite cranial massage.

⭐

Coolidge also kept various breeds of dogs and cats, canaries, a donkey, a bobcat, a goose, a bear, a wallaby, and lion cubs. For good measure, he added a pygmy hippo.

"No matter how much cats fight, there always seem to be plenty of kittens."

— *Abraham Lincoln*

A nearby cameraman once photographed Jimmy Carter as he battled a swamp rabbit that tried to board his boat during a fishing trip in Georgia. Swamp rabbits are herbivores.

One day, Benjamin Harrison chased the family goat, Whiskers, who had run off while pulling a cart full of the president's grandchildren.

★ ★ ★ ★ ★ ★ ★ ★ ★ ★ ★

Thomas Jefferson had two bear cubs that adventurers Lewis and Clark brought back from their journeys. Jefferson's pet mockingbird flew freely inside the White House unless the president had guests. It's not clear if the bear cubs were considered guests for the mockingbird's sake.

★

"You can put wings on a pig, but you don't make it an eagle."

— *Bill Clinton*

★

Soviet Union Premier Nikita Khrushchev gave Caroline Kennedy a puppy called Pushinka. Her mother Strelka was one of the first dogs in space. The pup was checked for bugs. Pushinka and Charlie the Welsh terrier had four puppies, or pupniks as President Kennedy called them.

A living horned toad was once placed into the cornerstone of a building in Texas as an informal experiment. Thirty-one years later, more than 3,000 people gathered. When the old cornerstone was opened and the dusty and apparently lifeless horned toad was held up, it began kicking a leg and looking for breakfast. Dubbed Old Rip, the horned toad lived another year, during which it toured the United States and received a formal audience with Calvin Coolidge.

★

Abraham Lincoln declared the official Thanksgiving holiday for the first time. But Lincoln's youngest son, Tad, adopted a turkey named Jack and trained the bird to eat from his hand and follow him around. When the holiday approached and Tad learned Jack's fate, he panicked. The boy burst into a cabinet meeting to

plead for Jack's life. (Lincoln also once wrote his own thank-you note to a citizen who sent some white rabbits for his children. Whether they were "pets or meat" — apologies to filmmaker Michael Moore — is a question for the ages.)

The Marquis de Lafayette once gave John Quincy Adams an alligator. If you weren't sure about someone, this is the kind of gift that'd move the marker more toward "frenemy." Maybe the Marquis knew of Adams's daily nude swims in the Potomac.

James Buchanan received a herd of elephants from the King of Siam.

Famous for his foreign diplomacy, Bill Clinton kept a dog and cat together in the White House. Socks the cat came with the Clinton family in 1993. Buddy, a chocolate Labrador retriever, arrived in 1997 as a gift. Upon leaving office, Clinton gave Socks to secretary Betty Currie and took Buddy with him to New York.

INFLATION

★

It's a safe guess that all presidents kept quite high opinions of themselves, at least at times. But most also kept those high opinions to themselves.

A few were caught speaking highly of themselves, and at least a couple of these remarks are self aware. John Adams: the original humblebraggart?

"By my physical constitution I am but an ordinary man ... Yet some great events, some cutting expressions, some mean hypocracies, have at times thrown this assemblage of sloth, sleep, and littleness into rage like a lion."

— *John Adams*

"After the long exercise of power, the ordinary affairs of life seem petty and commonplace. An ex-President practicing law or going into business is like a locomotive hauling a delivery wagon. He has lost his sense of proportion."

— *Grover Cleveland*

"You are uneasy; you never sailed with me before, I see."

— *Andrew Jackson, to an elderly fellow passenger*

"I'm the one who is doing all the work, so we just want you to stay cool for a minute."

— *John F. Kennedy, in his famous*
"We Choose to Go to the Moon" speech

MIXED
Blessings

These topics and remarks aren't quite cringeworthy but aren't quite accomplishments either. It turns out an ambivalent attitude toward presidency and the man in the office is as old as America itself.

Fortunately, most U.S. presidents didn't need to reason away their daytime napping.

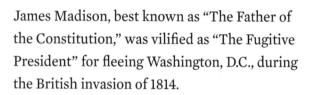

Jimmy Carter is a speed-reader, and has been recorded reading 2,000 words per minute.

James Madison, best known as "The Father of the Constitution," was vilified as "The Fugitive President" for fleeing Washington, D.C., during the British invasion of 1814.

"I was the only calm one in the house. You see I've been shot at by experts."

> — *Harry S. Truman,*
> *describing an assassination attempt*

Calvin Coolidge justified snoozing on the job by arguing that he couldn't initiate any costly federal programs while sleeping.

Benjamin Harrison was the first president to use electricity in the White House, but after getting an electrical shock, he refused to touch light switches, and he and his family would often leave the lights on all night.

Warren G. Harding sometimes answered the front door of the White House himself.

In 1931, the immense Boulder Dam on America's Colorado River was renamed the Hoover Dam. When Franklin D. Roosevelt defeated Hoover the next year, Congress changed the name back to Boulder Dam. After Roosevelt died, Congress changed the name back to Hoover Dam.

★

Gerald Ford is the only president since 1960 not to be featured on the cover of *MAD* magazine.

★

"The satisfaction arising from the indulgent opinion entertained by the American People of my conduct, will, I trust, be some security for preventing me from doing any thing, which might justly incur the forfeiture of that opinion."

— *George Washington*

Robert Frost wrote a poem for John F. Kennedy's presidential inauguration, but he couldn't read it through the sun's glare at the actual ceremony. He recited another poem from memory. James Garfield was wrong: Frost could have used someone from government to stand in his sunshine.

★

Gerald Ford was a male model in his youth. His work appeared in both *Life* and *Cosmopolitan* magazines.

★

"In getting Baker the nomination I shall be fixed a good deal like a fellow who is made a groomsman to a man that has cut him out and is marrying his own dear 'gal.'"

— *Abraham Lincoln*

"I love to deal with doctrines and events. The contests of men about men I greatly dislike."

— *James Garfield*

"He had a way of handling men so that they thought their ideas were his own."

— *Elihu Root, Secretary of War under William McKinley*

George W. Bush used his mildly derisive nickname, "Dubya," to tweak opponent Al Gore's self-alleged invention of the Internet, noting that he himself was referred to as "Dubya, Dubya, Dubya." The humor is . . . dubious.

★ ★ ★ ★ ★ ★ ★ ★ ★ ★ ★ ★

At Baylor Medical Center in Waco, hand surgeon Adrian Flatt has assembled dozens of bronze casts of famous people's hands. The collection includes numerous athletes, actors, and presidents. Jimmy Carter refused to remove his wedding ring for the casting, explaining that he never took it off. Of course, he also once told Playboy: "I've looked on many women with lust. I've committed adultery in my heart many times. God knows I will do this and forgives me."

★

On January 1, 1907, Theodore Roosevelt shook almost 9,000 hands — a record for the time.

★

Ronald Reagan is the only U.S. president to have a star on the Hollywood Walk of Fame.

Everyone in Lyndon B. Johnson's family had initials LBJ. His wife was nicknamed Lady Bird, and his daughters were Linda Bird and Lucy Baines. Even the family dog, Little Beagle Johnson, got in on the action.

★

George Washington was a world-renowned war hero and leader. But the only anecdote most people know about the first president is the infamous cherry tree legend, fabricated by a "biographer" who was concerned that Washington seemed too dull. Perhaps he was right: Washington's inaugural address was 31 pages long, and the original pages were later given away by a bored historian.

OUCH!

★

No one can criticize a president like another president. In fact, presidency offers a rare, near universal platform from which to throw shade.

It would be hard to match the historian who gave away the pages of George Washington's written inaugural address, but each president had moments of dubious praise, all-out mudslinging, or uncharitable comparisons.

Only two presidents, John Adams and his son, John Quincy Adams, did not attend the inauguration ceremonies of their successors.

★

"That man has offered me unsolicited advice for six years, all of it bad!"

— Calvin Coolidge on disgraced president Herbert Hoover

★

"If General McClellan does not want to use the army, I would like to borrow it for a time."

— Abraham Lincoln. McClellan didn't find out that President Lincoln had decided to remove him from the command of the Army of the Potomac until he read about it in a day-old newspaper.

"The Republican nominee-to-be, of course, is also a young man. But his approach is as old as McKinley. His party is the party of the past. His speeches are generalities from Poor Richard's Almanac."

— *John F. Kennedy, trashing Richard Nixon at the 1960 Democratic National Convention*

★

At one state dinner, a guest told "Silent Cal" Coolidge she had wagered friends that she could get at least three words out of the Sphinx of the Potomac. Coolidge replied, "You lose."

★

"You perhaps know that General Hardin and I have a contest for the Whig nomination for Congress for this district. He has had a turn and my argument is 'turn about is fair play.' I shall be pleased if this strikes you as a sufficient argument."

— *Abraham Lincoln*

⭐

"I would not for the world discredit any sort of philanthropy except the small and churlish sort which seeks to reform by nagging. [...] Are we to allow the poor personal habits of other people to absorb and quite use up all our fine indignation?"

— *Woodrow Wilson*

⭐

"His mind was great and powerful, without being of the very first order; his penetration strong, though, not so acute as that of a Newton, Bacon, or Locke; and as far as he saw, no judgment was ever sounder. It was slow in operation, being little aided by invention or imagination, but sure in conclusion."

— *Thomas Jefferson,*
"praising" George Washington

"My opponent now says he'll raise them as a last resort, or a third resort. But when a politician talks like that, you know that's one resort he'll be checking into."

— *George H.W. Bush*

"I believe that it was upon your recommendation that B. B. Bunker was appointed attorney for Nevada Territory. I am pressed to remove him on the ground that he does not attend to the office, nor in fact pass much time in the Territory. Do you wish to say anything on the subject?"

— *Abraham Lincoln*

"Mister Speaker, I am not able to understand the mental organization of the man who can consider this bill, and the subject of which it treats, as free from very great difficulties. He must be a man of very moderate abilities, whose ignorance is bliss, or a man of transcendent genius, whom no difficulties can daunt and whose clear vision no cloud can obscure."

— *James Garfield*

"Repetition does not transform a lie into a truth."

— *Franklin D. Roosevelt*

"I hope to have your hearty co-operation in carrying out its measures. So long as you see fit to do this, I shall be glad to have you with me. When you think otherwise, your resignations will be accepted."

— *John Tyler*

"We've gotta name this condition that he's going though. I think it's called Romnesia."

— *Barack Obama on Governor Mitt Romney's rapidly "evolving" policy positions*

"A lively and lasting sense of filial duty is more effectually impressed on the mind of a son or daughter by reading King Lear, than by all the dry volumes of ethics, and divinity, that ever were written."

> — *Thomas Jefferson. And he would know: When the British burned down the Capitol, including the original Library of Congress, President Jefferson's personal collection of 6,500 books seeded the replacement.*

"What astonishing changes a few years are capable of producing! I am told that even respectable characters speak of a monarchical form of government without horror."

> — *George Washington*

"By the way, I've been called worse on the basketball court. It's not a big deal."

— Barack Obama, responding to the far-flung insults of 2008 vice presidential candidate Sarah Palin

★

"I am glad to have the opportunity of standing up against a rabble of men who hasten to make weathercocks of themselves."

— James Garfield

★

"It's probably better to have him inside the tent pissing out, than outside the tent pissing in."

— Lyndon B. Johnson, on controversial FBI Director J. Edgar Hoover

"McKinley has no more backbone than a chocolate eclair."

— Theodore Roosevelt

★

"Nobody really thinks that Bush or McCain have a real answer for the challenges we face. So what they are going to try to do is make you scared of me. You know he — oh, he's not patriotic enough. He's got a funny name. You know, he doesn't look like all of those other presidents on those dollar bills."

— Barack Obama

★

"Do you realize the responsibility I carry? I'm the only person standing between Richard Nixon and the White House."

— John F. Kennedy

"What this country needs is a great poem. John Brown's Body was a step in the right direction. I've read it once, and I'm reading it again. But it's too long to do what I mean. You can't thrill people in 300 pages... The limit is about 300 words."

— Herbert Hoover

"The military circles are interested in the same things with myself, and so we endure, if not enjoy, each other."

— Rutherford B. Hayes

"Their number is negligible and they are stupid."

— Dwight Eisenhower on fringe opponents

ON CLEVELAND
Pond

★

One of American history's least discussed presidents spent his downtime writing prescriptive thoughts on hunting and fishing.

Grover Cleveland was the preeminent fiscal conservative in an era of massive financial change and upheaval in American politics — when he describes needing a break from the namecalling and complicated work, we can believe it.

The simple hard work of learning to be a great fisherman makes sense for a small-c conservative.

Grover Cleveland's political career had a unique respite: the four years between his discrete terms as president. His young wife Frances bore the first two of the family's five children during this time, and Cleveland discovered a fanatical love of fishing. His hobby reached a zenith when he published a book of his thoughts about the outdoor arts.

There aren't many common threads to pull between Cleveland and his contemporary Theodore Roosevelt, but they share an earnest love of sport and a belief in its curative, educational powers. Cleveland throws in a lot of prescriptive sass, too.

"Thus, when short fishing excursions, in which I have sought relief from the wearing labors and perplexities of official duty, have

been denounced in a mendacious newspaper as dishonest devices to cover scandalous revelry, I have been able to enjoy a sort of pleasurable contempt for the author of this accusation, while congratulating myself on the mental and physical restoration I had derived from these excursions."

— *Grover Cleveland*

"Not many years ago, while residing in a non-sporting but delightfully cultured and refined community, I found that considerable indignation had been aroused among certain good neighbors and friends, because it had been said of me that I was willing to associate in the field with any loafer who was the owner of a dog and gun."

— *Grover Cleveland*

"Men, in disobedience of this law, may achieve triumph in the world of science, education and art; but how unsatisfying are the rewards thus gained if they hasten the night when no man can work, and if the later hours of life are haunted by futile regrets for what is still left undone, that might have been done if there had been closer communion with nature's visible forms!"

— *Grover Cleveland*

"It must, of course, be admitted that large stories of fishing adventure are sometimes told by fishermen — and why should this not be so? Beyond all question there is no sphere of human activity so full of strange and wonderful incidents as theirs. Fish

are constantly doing the most mysterious and startling things; and no one has yet been wise enough to explain their ways or account for their conduct."

— *Grover Cleveland*

"This is perfectly understood by listening fishermen; and they, to their enjoyment and edification, are permitted by a properly adjusted mental equipment to believe what they hear."

— *Grover Cleveland*

"[W]hen the largest trout of the day, after a long struggle, winds the leader about a snag and escapes, [...] the

fisherman's code of morals will not condemn beyond forgiveness the holder of the straightened rod if he impulsively, but with all the gentility at his command, exclaims: 'Damn that fish!'"

— *Grover Cleveland*

"It is known of all men that one of the rudiments in the education of a true fisherman is the lesson of patience. If he has a natural tendency in this direction it must be cultivated. If such a tendency is lacking he must acquire patience by hard schooling."

— *Grover Cleveland*

PARTY
Time

Now that you've brushed up on Grover Cleveland's love of the outdoors, let's visit the spirit of party politics that drove him into a rowboat in the middle of nowhere in the first place.

Bill Clinton's speech at the 2012 Democratic National Convention helped to cement his legacy as the party mudslinger of his generation. But verbal violence between parties is as old as the nation itself.

"Conservatism is the policy of making no changes and consulting your grandmother when in doubt."

— *Woodrow Wilson*

"One of the commonplace charges of Mr. Cleveland's opponents among those of his own political faith is that he wrecked his party. It would be more nearly correct to say that the party wrecked itself."

— *New York* World

"And I admire that about the Republicans: The evidence does not faze them."

— *Bill Clinton*

"I hope you're all Republican."

> — *Ronald Reagan, joking with his*
> *surgical team after being shot*

"A radical is a man with both feet firmly planted in the air. A conservative is a man with two perfectly good legs who, however, has never learned to walk forward. A reactionary is a somnambulist walking backwards. A liberal is a man who uses his legs and his hands at the behest — at the command — of his head."

> — *Franklin D. Roosevelt*

"What a pleasant lot of fellows they are. What a pity they have so little sense about politics. If they lived North the last one of them would be Republicans."

— *Chester A. Arthur*

"My dog Millie knows more about foreign affairs than these two bozos."

— *George H.W. Bush, assessing the skillsets of Bill Clinton and Al Gore*

"And I am proud of the contrast with our Republican competitors. For their ranks are apparently so thin that not one challenger has come forth with both the competence and the courage to make theirs an open convention."

— *John F. Kennedy*

"We have seen none of 'the horrors' so often described, but on the other hand I have seen nothing to change my Northern opinions."

> — *Rutherford B. Hayes,*
> *spending time in Texas during the Civil War*

"When you see all that rhetorical smoke billowing up from the Democrats, well, ladies and gentleman, I'd follow the example of their nominee; don't inhale."

> — *Ronald Reagan, conjuring Bill Clinton's*
> *claim that he "didn't inhale" during his*
> *only experiment with marijuana*

"There's never a perfect bipartisan bill in the eyes of a partisan."

> — *Bill Clinton*

"When the chips are down and the decisions are made as to who the candidates will be, then the 11th commandment prevails and everybody goes to work, and that is: Thou shalt not speak ill of another Republican."

> — *Ronald Reagan. Interesting enough,*
> *President Reagan was a Democrat*
> *through much of the 1950s.*

"A conservative is a man who just sits and thinks; mostly sits."

> — *Woodrow Wilson*

"It always helps the right when people are insecure."

> — *Bill Clinton*

HATS OFF

★

Young, charismatic, and bold, John F. Kennedy spoke in sweeping sea-to-shining-sea-isms that helped propel postwar America into a time of great prosperity, advancement of knowledge, and power.

His legacy is debated with great energy: Was he a good president or is he famous for his good looks and shocking assassination?

But one thing is for certain: Kennedy had a lasting impact on hats. Yes, hats.

John F. Kennedy sparked a surprisingly durable rumor when he did not wear a hat to his inauguration. His choice coincided with the continued decline of the hat, which shrank in the 20th century from de rigueur to baseball caps in restaurants. Was Kennedy's slight indeed one small step for hats, one giant leap for hatkind?

The truth is that Kennedy wasn't wearing a hat when he took the pledge, but he wore a fine silk hat for much of the rest of the day both before and after. Kennedy didn't like hats and avoided wearing them when he could. He felt they made him look too old, and as the youngest-ever U.S. president and strong mobilizer of the liberal youth vote, he wanted to keep his image young and vital.

Dwight D. Eisenhower didn't wear a hat for the majority of his first inauguration ceremony, and it didn't seem to cause any kind of a fracas. If politicians had that sort of influence on fashion, Barack Obama, who often appears in public wearing an open-neck shirt, could singlehandedly ruin the tie industry. But the navy-blue bag suit and red or maroon tie persists as the unfashionable unofficial uniform of modern U.S. politics.

There's an entire book dedicated to debunking the myth that President Kennedy caused the downfall of the derby. In his book *Hatless Jack*, journalist

Neil Steinberg confirms that fashion is indeed fickle. Of course, books upon books are written about the clothing choices of first ladies and women politicians.

LEISURE
Time

★

Baseball is the national pastime and presidents have had a close relationship with the game since it began. But presidents' pursuit of leisure in all its forms dates back to George Washington's expensive appetite, Thomas Jefferson's extramarital activities, or John Quincy Adams's nude swims.

Let's focus on the more wholesome pastimes.

"Nolan [Ryan] says throw it high because amateurs get out there, no matter how good they are, and throw it in the dirt. You get more of an 'ooooh' if you heave it over the [catcher's] head instead of going with the fast-breaking deuce into the dirt."

— *George W. Bush*

★

Woodrow Wilson played golf as a source of exercise, even in winter. He had his golf balls painted red so he could see them in the snow. In contrast, Dwight Eisenhower requested that a tree at Augusta National be removed because it was interfering with his drives.

★

Lyndon B. Johnson loved driving — specifically drunk driving on his Texas ranch in a specially designed amphibious convertible. Johnson would feign brake failure and plunge his magic car into the nearest body of water, taking his unsuspecting passengers with him.

★

"I have read your lousy review of Margaret's concert. I've come to the conclusion that you are an eight ulcer man on a four ulcer job ... Some day I hope to meet you. When that happens you'll need a new nose, a lot of beefsteak for black eyes and perhaps a supporter below."

— *Harry S. Truman, following*
one of his daughter's vocal concerts

★

At the 1976 All-Star Game, the athletic Gerald Ford thrilled fans by throwing one pitch right-handed to Johnny Bench of the Cincinnati Reds and a second pitch left-handed to Carlton Fisk of the Boston Red Sox.

Of course, President James Garfield could write Latin with one hand and Greek with the other — at the same time. But that will never earn you a $72 million contract.

"Now, before I begin, I'd just like to clear the air about that little controversy everybody was talking about a few weeks back. I have to tell you, I really thought this was much ado about nothing, but I do think we all learned an important lesson. I learned never again to pick another team over the Sun Devils in my NCAA brackets. It won't happen again."

— *Barack Obama, speaking at Arizona State University*

★

"I like to see Quentin practicing baseball. It gives me hope that one of my boys will not take after his father in this respect, and will prove able to play the national game."

— *Theodore Roosevelt*

★

In 1972, Ryan O'Malley founded a yacht club for people with yachts — and those without. The Cornucopia Yacht Club didn't even host any aquatic events. Anyone could join, and hundreds did, including President Gerald Ford. Applicants had to answer only one question: "What is the name of your boat, and if you don't have one, what would you call it?"

At the Lyndon B. Johnson Presidential Library, In addition to serious historical memorabilia, visitors can meet an animated, life-size figure of Johnson that's dressed in a Western shirt and cowboy hat and tells jokes.

"A couple of years ago, they told me I was too young to be President and you were too old to be playing baseball. But we fooled them."

> — *45-year-old John F. Kennedy to 41-year-old Stan Musial at the 1962 All-Star Game*

"I don't know a lot about politics, but I know a lot about baseball."

> — *Richard Nixon*

CHEAP SHOTS

★

Even U.S. presidents ham it up once in a while, or sometimes more than once in a while — looking at you, Gerald Ford and Ronald Reagan.

In a comedy club, these zingers would be followed by the prompt of a drum hit and, if there were a two-drink minimum, maybe a laugh.

It's hard to be funny, and it's hard to be president. Draw your own conclusions.

"I have often wanted to drown my troubles, but I can't get my wife to go swimming."

— *Jimmy Carter*

⭐

"The three-martini lunch is the epitome of American efficiency. Where else can you get an earful, a bellyful and a snootful at the same time?"

— *Gerald Ford*

⭐

"I have only one thing to say to the tax increasers: Go ahead, make my day."

— *Ronald Reagan*

"A friend of mine and I went fishing and as we sat there in the warmth of the summer afternoon on a river bank, we talked about what we wanted to do when we grew up. I told him that I wanted to be a real major league baseball player, a genuine professional like Honus Wagner. My friend said that he'd like to be President of the United States. Neither of us got our wish."

— *Dwight Eisenhower*

"A mob is a body of men in hot contact with one another, moved by ungovernable passion to do a hasty thing that they will regret the next day."

— *Woodrow Wilson*

"Now I have something I can give everybody."

— *Abraham Lincoln, who came*
down with contagious, mild smallpox
after the Gettysburg Address

★

"If humor be the safety of our race, then it is due largely to the infusion into the American people of the Irish brain."

— *William Howard Taft*

★

"I am reminded every day of my life, if not by events, then by my wife, that I am not a perfect man."

— *Barack Obama*

"We're going to keep trying to strengthen the American family. To make them more like the Waltons and less like the Simpsons."

— *George H.W. Bush*

"Making a speech on economics is a lot like pissing down your leg. It seems hot to you, but it never does to anyone else."

— *Lyndon B. Johnson*

"Look, when I was a kid, I inhaled frequently. That was the point."

— *Barack Obama, conjuring Bill Clinton's claim that he "didn't inhale" during his only experiment with marijuana*

"Reagan doesn't have that presidential look."

— United Artists film executive

"John Calhoun, if you secede from my nation I will secede your head from the rest of your body."

— Andrew Jackson

"My name is Jimmy Carter, and I'm not running for president."

— Jimmy Carter,
at the 2004 Democratic National Convention

"You know, if I were a single man, I might ask that mummy out. That's a good-looking mummy."

— Bill Clinton

"Mr. Nixon may feel it is his turn now, after the New Deal and the Fair Deal – but before he deals, someone had better cut the cards."

— John F. Kennedy, at the 1960 Democratic National Convention

"I am not a crook."

— Richard Nixon

"Obviously, it's a great privilege and pleasure to be here at the Yale Law School Sesquicentennial Convocation. And I defy anyone to say that and chew gum at the same time."

— *Gerald Ford*

"This university has been coeducational since 1870, but I do not believe it was on the basis of your accomplishments that a Detroit high school girl said, 'In choosing a college, you first have to decide whether you want a coeducational school or an educational school.' Well, we can find both here at Michigan, although perhaps at different hours."

— *Lyndon B. Johnson*

CIVILLY
Disobedient

Abraham Lincoln was one of the greatest presidents in U.S. history for his devoted, self-sacrificing leadership during the Civil War. But he was also a world-famous story- and joke-teller with a natural knack for comedy.

The relentless stress of his political and personal life only increased the need for a sense of humor. Lincoln was a gifted writer and communicator whose talent for words lent itself to his dry wit.

Presidential humor begins and ends with Abraham Lincoln, whose one-liners alone could fill a volume. Lincoln's humor was rich and smart but never snobby. He wanted to be liked and respected, and he practiced the Golden Rule. Barack Obama cites Lincoln as one of his more special influences, visible in Obama's almost relentless use of analogies and other more "regular" language. But from Lincoln it flowed naturally.

His life's correspondence — public remarks, letters, telegrams, and transcripts — fill seven volumes. Even in the darkest moments of the Civil War or his family tragedies, Lincoln was gracious and funny to all who crossed his path. He was sometimes less so to those who crossed him personally.

"I have no speech to make to you; and no time to speak in. I appear before you that I may see you, and that you may see me; and I am willing to admit that so far as the ladies are concerned I have the best of the bargain, though I wish it to be understood that I do not make the same acknowledgment concerning the men."

— *Abraham Lincoln, to a waiting crowd at a campaign stop in New York*

★

"MY DEAR SIR: — Herewith is the diplomatic address and my reply. To whom the reply should be addressed — that is, by what title or style — I do not quite understand, and therefore I have left it blank."

— *Abraham Lincoln*

"That part of the country is within itself as unpoetical as any spot on earth; but still seeing it and its objects and inhabitants aroused feelings in me which were certainly poetry; though whether my expression of these feelings is poetry, is quite another question."

— *Abraham Lincoln, belying his own status as one of U.S. history's most eloquent, heartfelt speakers*

"I certainly know that if the war fails the administration fails, and that I will be blamed for it, whether I deserve it or not. And I ought to be blamed if I could do better. You think I could do better; therefore you blame me already. I think I could not do better; therefore I blame you for blaming me."

— Abraham Lincoln, responding to General Carl Schurz's 1862 accusation that Lincoln was failing as the commander of Union forces

★

"I appreciate him certainly, as highly as you do; but you can never know until you have the trial, how difficult it is to find a place for an officer of so high rank when there is no place seeking him."

— Abraham Lincoln, explaining to Andrew Johnson in 1864 why he could not find employment for Schurz

"I think I can answer the Judge [Douglas] so long as he sticks to the premises; but when he flies from them, I cannot work any argument into the consistency of a mental gag and actually close his mouth with it."

— *Abraham Lincoln, who stood a full foot taller than Stephen Douglas even without his hat*

★

"Logan is worse beaten than any other man ever was since elections were invented."

— *Abraham Lincoln*

★

"I shall prefer emigrating to some country where they make no pretense of loving liberty, — to Russia, for instance, where despotism can be taken pure, and without the base alloy of hypocrisy."

— *Abraham Lincoln*

"This is not a long letter, but it contains the whole story."

— Abraham Lincoln

"We hold these truths to be self-evident, that all British subjects who were on this continent eighty-one years ago were created equal to all British subjects born and then residing in Great Britain."

— Abraham Lincoln, mocking Stephen Douglas in a debate. Douglas claimed that the Declaration of Independence intended only to clarify that British citizens now living in the United States were "created equal" to British citizens living in the United Kingdom.

"You don't know what you are talking about, my friend. I am quite willing to answer any gentleman in the crowd who asks an intelligent question."

> — *Abraham Lincoln,*
> *addressing a rowdy audience member*

"A decision of the court is to him a 'Thus saith the Lord.'"

> — *Abraham Lincoln*

FOOD TALK

★

President George H.W. Bush holds the "honor" of most famous presidential food anecdote with his refutation of the very idea of broccoli. But did you know Bill Clinton was allergic to multiple parts of his beloved cheeseburgers?

Food plays the same huge role in White House life that it does in civilian life. Clinton didn't corner the market on dairy topics, either. Who knew Andrew Jackson's taste in cheese was so . . . cultured?

Credit for America's French-fry fondness goes to Thomas Jefferson, who sampled the thinly sliced, fried potatoes as an ambassador to France. He brought the delicacy home, serving "potatoes, fried in the French manner" at an 1801 or 1802 White House dinner.

"Has it not got down as thin as the homeopathic soup that was made by boiling the shadow of a pigeon that had starved to death?"

— *Abraham Lincoln*

In 1802, a cheesemaker delivered a 1,235-pound wheel of cheese to Thomas Jefferson. Citizens declared it the "big cheese," referring to both the wheel and its important recipient.

In 1835, a different cheesemaker delivered a 1,400-pound wheel of cheddar to Andrew Jackson. The appreciative president, whose love of cheese was well known, gave Meacham a dozen bottles of wine and his hearty thanks. At the order of the president, the cheese was allowed to age for two years in the White House lobby. According to historians, Jackson served the cheese at a White House party.

"I do not like broccoli. And I haven't liked it since I was a little kid and my mother made me eat it. And I'm president of the United States and I'm not going to eat any more broccoli. Now look, this is the last statement I'm going to have on broccoli. There are truckloads of broccoli at this very minute descending on Washington. My family is divided. For the broccoli vote out there: Barbara loves broccoli. She has tried to make me eat it. She eats it all the time herself. So she can go out and meet the caravan of broccoli that's coming in."

— *George H.W. Bush*

In 1996, Bill Clinton signed the Popcorn Promotion, Research, and Consumer Information Act, leading to the formation of the National Popcorn Board.

"I wish some of you would tell me the brand of whiskey that Grant drinks. I would like to send a barrel of it to my other generals."

— *Abraham Lincoln*

★

"In 1777, largely, it seems, because he refused to treat the electors with rum and punch, after the custom of the time, he was not re-elected."

— *the 1911* Encyclopedia Britannica
entry for James Madison

★

President George W. Bush choked on a pretzel and lost consciousness while watching the 2002 Baltimore–Miami NFL playoff game in the White House.

Early in his presidency, Bill Clinton suffered from a series of allergies including cat dander, beef, milk, mold spores, and weed and grass pollens. He took injections to control the allergies, which allowed him to partake in a favorite food at the time: cheeseburgers.

"Broken eggs cannot be mended."

— *Abraham Lincoln*